As the days turn into nigh
why God?

This morning I dreamt I was putting a Babylonian Muslim in their place. I was so angry at him in the dream I told him he stole black people's history and say it's theirs.

I asked him what Allah means and he could not tell me so I told him what Allah meant. I schooled him Lovey and all he could do was shut his mouth and say nothing.

I told him they (Muslims) disrespected God; you Lovey with their killings; murders. Man was I ever upset; mad. Thus I am asking you Lovey; WHY?

I have to ask you why because I see the religious and political murders; killings here on earth and I am disheartened by it. Disheartened that humans use god and gods including idols as tools to carry out their murderous tendencies.

Disheartened that humans use religion and politics to lie and deceive; kill.

Disheartened that humans use you as a pawn in their ponzi schemes Lovey.

Man say; there are only Ten Commandments, but if you count them (the commandments) as written in man's so called holy book; bible, you will find more than Ten

Commandments. We say, _**"thou shalt not kill,"**_ but daily you have people breaking this commandment; killing.

You have men fighting and killing for land.

You have men fighting and killing for political dictatorship.

You have men fighting and killing for religious dominance and control.

You have religious men and women including children fornicating whilst they say they are of you and they are spreading your message. All this they do behind their pulpits whist standing before you God and man; congregation. Thus defiling self before you God and Man.

You have men including pastors and deacons that knowing have HIV and AIDS that say they are of you God and knowingly sleep with their congregation including others in and out of the church and infecting them with their disease.

You have men and women including children robbing the church of the tides and offerings given to them by their congregation and others.

So now tell me Lovey, _**Why?**_

Is this truly you, what you wanted for humans?

Is the lies and deceit of these men and women worth it?

Why let humans degrade you like this?

Why let humans tell lies on you like this?

Why see the lies and disgrace of men and women including children when it comes to humans and continue to step aside and let dirty people; man, woman and child destroy you, your goodness?

No, today I will not yell and be harsh because of my Babylonian dream. I cannot because I schooled him in the spiritual realm already. But I am concerned about you Lovey and the lies men and women tell when it comes to you.

I KNOW THESE PEOPLE ARE NOT YOUR TRUE PEOPLE, BUT WHY LET THEM DECEIVE HUMANITY LIKE THIS?

Why let them take billions to hell especially the black race?

Everywhere the devil and his people go, they set up shop and shape the landscape of earth with their Mosques and Terror; Violence, Lies and Deceit; Death.

Why let them tag along Lovey?

I know you don't listen to me but I've told you, I want nor do I need any of them (Babylonians) in our world and or kingdom. No strays Lovey because they destroy the natural beauty of life all around. They are not clean people nor are they beautiful in my book; so truly keep them the hell away from me and our good and true people including land and lands.

You know my truth hence they are more than infinitely and indefinitely locked out more than forever ever without end. This is my true good will Lovey. *You cannot destroy a race of people including their home; land of truth like that and expect to get away with it. You cannot come into our good up good up home and destroy us like that; cause our beloved and truth of life and more than protection to flee from us. You truly do not like humanity thus you give humanity lies to keep us from life.*

You are dead, so you want us to become dead like you also. No, this cannot work. Life is truly not about death. Life, good and true life is about truth and cleanliness come on now.

Tell me Lovey, how can anyone say they are of you but yet destroy their fellow humans just like that?

How can another human being knowingly and willingly destroy another human life just like that?

You say you are of God but yet all that God told you not to do, you do. Some of you use the name of God to fornicate; have sexual intercourse with members of your congregation including others.

You use the name of God for money and sexual favours. Money that was meant to help your congregation and others (community), you use for your own personal benefit; gain.

Now tell me, how can any of you say you are of God and dirt surrounds you?

You are not clean but yet you stand before God and man professing your cleanliness and self worth and you Lovey let them.

Man; humans have and has destroyed your credibility; thus I told you Lovey, you have no credit here on earth.

Humans have and has ruined you, and in the process ruined self due to greed and money; lies and deceit.

So what say you Lovey?
Truly what say you?

Yes it's Saturday November 12, 2015 and I am listening to some soothing music by Christopher Martin.

Wow because this youth is so good musically. We so need to get back into the groove of singing clean and wholesome music when it comes to reggae and cultural music.

NA NA NA by Christopher Martin, big tune. Big up yourself youth, mi rate yu music.

As I think of my readers I dedicate this song (NA NA NA) to all of you and if we could get together, I would lay all of you on my chest to sleep; cuddle. You are my preferred and rather; so let me hook you with my truth and true love of truth for all of you. One day I will dance with you all to this song. So keep me strong and in truth with all of you. You had better lest I be upset with the lots of you seriously. When you see me going wrong, correct me because you are all my rod and rods of correction and hope. True love always, so truly fall in truth and true love with me always. Truly listen to this song because it's our dedication on this day.

Come on, truly let me think of you over and over again because my truth and true love for all of you is truly true and more than divine.

Ah my true loved ones. Be my truth because we are more than living in serious times right now and I truly need to save you, so listen to true counsel. If you feel I am wrong tell me I am wrong and why I am wrong. We are free and we are living in a free society of cleanliness and truth. So never lie to me nor deceive me. Like I said, you are my preferred and rather, so stay preferred and rather with me because you have a true saving grace with me. I know I cannot save your flesh, but I know I can save your spirit in the after world. So stay close to

me please. Take my hand and let's walk together in truth, true love, honesty and true peace. Know that I am not here to deceive you, thus my goodness is shared with you also all around. And yes, if I could save your flesh I would as long as you are good and true.

Onwards I go because I know some of you are going to find this book confusing and hard to follow on some level.

It's amazing how we say we love God; we're Christians, Protestants, Muslims, Jehovah's Witness, Jews, Catholics, Anglican, Baptist, Seventh Day Adventist, and what have you, but yet go on the battlefield of death and kill each other for what?

What are we killing each other for?
What are we hating and destroying each other for?

If we say God is at the head of our home; life and household, should we not let God be at the head of our home; life and household and not death?

Some of you say you are a pastor, but yet you fornicate with this member and that member of your church including outside of your church.

Now tell me this, HOW CLEAN IS GOD'S HOUSE; THE HOUSE YOU GAVE TO GOD IF YOU ARE SHELLING DOWN SISTER PAT, SISTER ANNE,

BROTHER WILKINS, BROTHER JENKINS, SISTER WRIGHT AND BROTHER WRIGHT INSIDE THE CHURCH YOU SAY IS GOD'S CHURCH AND OR OF GOD?

You are having sex in the house of God and people are to say God is clean when you do this?

People are to accept God, your nasty god when this is happening? You are having sexual intercourse in the church, so how clean is your church and God?

Nigger Bitch you are fucking in the church of God and exchanging bodily fluids and God; Lovey is to accept a nasty fuck like you???

Please you nasty slut and slut dog.

Tell me something, when you have sexual intercourse in a church; HAVE YOU NOT DIRTIED GOD'S CHURCH?

HAVE YOU NOT MADE GOD AS DIRTY, FILTHY AND NASTY AS YOU?

SO, HOW CAN GOD SAVE ANY OF YOU NASTY BITCHES? You discredit him on all levels come on now.

<u>You put him on the same nasty level as you.</u>

<u>How can God be with any of you if you've defiled the premise of cleanliness and truth?</u>

YOU ARE A VIOLATION OF LIFE. So now tell me how can PEOPLE TRUST THE CLERGY, WHEN THE CLERGY DEFILE AND CONDEMN THE REALM OF CLEANLINESS; LOVEY, GOOD GOD AND ALLELUJAH ALL AROUND?

You've wronged God with your nastiness and lies. You use religion and God as a pawn; thus defiling self and your followers; congregations. So because of this, your congregation is condemned alongside you. They participate in nastiness alongside you, so their names are written in death's book with yours. They are literally hell bound with you and there isn't a damned thing they can do about it. They (your congregation) willingly and knowingly participate in the violation of God, Good God and Allelujah; Lovey. They (your congregation) willingly and knowingly accept lies and nastiness thus condemning self all around.

Wow because many of you are going to feel it for the lies and wrongs you've done to Lovey. I truly don't want to be any of you because your hell is a greater hell than hell. You tell lies on God himself, so what say the lots of you when death comes a knocking and a calling for you? Some a unnu say; this is God's church and wuk obeah and voodoo in the same church you dedicate onto God and call holy.

Some of you molest little boys and girls; so tell me, *how clean have you made God?*

More importantly, how clean have you kept God?

All that you've said is for God; you've dirtied and kept dirty. You shame God and put God to shame. Now think of forgiveness. How can Lovey and or God forgive any of you when you defame and slander his name and character so?

Yes it's Saturday and I am thinking of Lovey and my Mother, and as I dance with my mother and Lovey; I dedicate SWEET SWEET LOVE by Christopher Martin to the both of you. The both of you are my sweet sweet love and more than treasure. You are both my hope and ray of sunlight each and every day. And as I think of the both of you while listening to this song, know that the both of you are my unconditional. *You are both my songs and songs of praise and joy, and no matter what IT IS YOU; THE BOTH OF YOU FOR MORE THAN LIFE ETERNAL AND EVER AFTER.*

All that is my truth and true love is you; the both of you. Know that truth will forever reign with us. So as I make sweet sweet love of truth in words, my dance, my food, sleep, waking days and hours including nights, my speech, health, wealth, hair, breath, walk, talk; all, continue to be my preferred treasure and rather here on earth and in the spiritual world. You are thought of and will always be truly loved by me.

KNOW THAT IF THE BOTH OF YOU NEED A BEACON OF LIGHT I WILL BE THAT BEACON OF LIGHT, LIFE AND HOPE. I more than cherish the both of you and I too am missing the both of you. Please take my hand as I take yours and let's continue to walk in truth and true love together. Never forget that the both of you are my unconditional; more than conditional because you're both a part of my good and true life all around.

Mother and Father, truly thank you and truly forgive me on this day for my mistakes and problems given to the both of you in the spiritual and physical world.

Thank you for being a part of my true and good world more than forever more unconditionally.

Lovey it's a shame that people had to defame you like this with their lies, but I know there is an APP for them and that is HELL; a GREATER HELL THAN MAN KNOWS.

You do not say your bible is holy and from God and walk on the road of lies and deceit come on now. Yes I know it's hard, but you Lovey do make a way for us no matter how small it is.

11

Coming to you is not hard Lovey; I know this. It took me a while to trust you but in all I did, I made you my doubt and hope, truth and true love including beating stick.

I do get down on you and I am truly glad I do this. Truly thank you for taking me out of the church and churches of the wicked. Thus Psalms One told us to keep away from the counsel of the wicked. They are not looked upon by you Lovey.

There is no forgiveness for these wicked and evil people because THEY LIED AGAINST YOU LOVEY. THEY WILLINGLY AND WILLFULLY DECEIVE HUMANITY FOR PROFIT WHOOPS PROPHET.

Lovey I am going to ask again, because I've asked you this in other books. ***What does it profit a man to tell lies on you and lose his soul?***

You are the creator and someone lies on you like this Lovey? Do they not know what they have done?

Do they not know hell here in the living and in the grave?

Do they not care about life including your life Lovey?

Do they not know the hell they are going to face?

Do they not know their grave and hell in the grave?

Lovey, these people claim they are holy but yet go against cleanliness.

Yet I ask again, what good is anyone that willingly and willfully; knowingly tell lies on you?

How can you provide them a true home Lovey?

How can you truly save them when they deceive humanity and keep all in humanity away from you?

Their lies and deceit have and has kept you from this earth; thus contributing more to the sins of this earth and universe.

Lovey, how can you know these people that have and has turned humanity against you?

Now tell me Lovey, *HOW CAN YOU SAVE HUMANITY WHEN HUMANITY; HUMANS ARE UNCLEAN?*

How can you save humanity knowing the vile sins of us humans?

How can we say you are our god and saviour when we constantly sin and defile the law and laws of good and true life?

Lovey, look at the sins of humans including mine. I will not take myself out of this despite you asking me to write you a book. I too have sinned like all in humanity and despite me asking you for forgiveness, it does not change the fact that I have sinned in my book.

Yes I am learning about you and I do know you, but you did hurt. I did hurt you including my mother and now her flesh is gone. I know she is with you, but I did hurt her. Now I seek her forgiveness is some way but cannot get her forgiveness, her flesh is not with me. She's a spiritual being now and I've yet to see her tell me that I am forgiven for all the trouble I gave her in the living.

Man do I regret giving her so much talking, well not a lot but in any way, I did give her talking. Some of us do not know the good counselling of our parents and this is sad.

Is it too late to learn?

No, it's not.

If your parents are still alive and they are counselling you the right and proper way then learn to listen. Yes it's hard and will be hard, but take your time and take it one step at a time each and every day. You will fuss and mutter under your breath and this is fine, but know that YOUR GOOD PARENT AND OR PARENTS ARE SECURING YOUR GOOD AND TRUE FUTURE SO THAT

*WHEN YOU HAVE CHILDREN, YOU DO NOT SUFFER
WITH THEM.*

I suffer with mine but you know what, my pain is truly
not suffering. I learn from my children. They too want to
experience life and or things on their own and I let
them. I am clingy to my children and I have to stop
being clingy. They are saying to me mommy, I want to
learn for myself now. Yes it's hard for me to let go
because I feel I have always protect them. Yes they are
of age and old enough but I have to let go because the
disrespect is there; attitude. Some of their friends I truly
do not want to see at my house each and every day. You
know the spirit and some of the spirit is truly not clean;
dark. So I truly don't want to see them each and every
day. I don't want them coming to my place.

And as I look at my life, I realize I do not have it hard as
some other parents. No, I am not comparing and I refuse
to compare my life with anyone because your life is
truly not mine and my life is truly not yours. My
struggles are my struggles and I have to face them until
I am out. If you've read some of my other books that talk
about my children, you see and know my hardships and
struggles not just with them but with me.

Never ever compare you with others under any
circumstances. Yes you see the struggles of others but
never ever compare yourself to someone else do you
hear me. Some people treated their parents like crap
and they are feeling it.

Some people, other people create hell for them in their lives.

Some people are just living breathing demons in the flesh here on earth. Their soul and or sole purpose is to make your life hell in the harshest and brutalest of ways.

Some people carry generational sins and or curse on them here in the living. Thus this curse goes from generation to generation and cannot be expunged.

Some of us got the message from Lovey and ignored it; went full throttle into the relationship and now you are paying the price for it. I know this one because in truth some of us truly do not know the way Lovey speaks to us and show us things. I didn't, thus I learnt the hard way and now I tell you and teach you to listen to Lovey because the brutality of sin is more than a bitch here on earth. Trust me, I truly do not want to go to hell and pay for my sins.

So if you have good parents securing you, truly learn to listen and obey. I know what my mother was saying now and I truly cherish her for this; her truth and wisdom. And although I do not have her in the flesh, I have her in the spirit. She is with me just like Lovey is. Yes I know some parents are bitch niggas, but you will get over. Remember you are growing and in a couple of years or few you, will be out of the negative environment you are in. You are living and in many ways the evil that surrounds you is dying. Evil hath time but life, true life is truly forever ever without end. So worry not about your enemies. All they do must come to an end one day. Some of you live to see them (your enemies) crumble in the living only for them (your enemies) to go to hell and spend billions, hundreds of billions of years including trillions and hundreds of trillions of years in hell's fire. And this matters not if the person is in the grave. One is waiting in hell while the other is resting in true peace with Lovey.

To some of you hell is no consolation, but trust me let it be. Death cannot show you their abode because they (Death) want to keep you sinning so that you can keep them alive in hell longer. Each soul and or spirit death gets add up for death; meaning the longer it takes death to die. WE AS HUMANS KEEP DEATH ALIVE NOT THE OTHER WAY AROUND. Come on now.

DEATH NEEDS YOU NOT YOU NEED DEATH.

So if you have good and true parents and or parent, hug them and tell them you are sorry for all the trouble you've given them. Beg their forgiveness in truth so that when you grow older your life can be good. ***IT DOES NOT MEAN YOU WON'T HAVE TROUBLE IN YOUR LIFE, BUT IT WILL NOT BE SO SEVERE.*** Trust me the brutality of sin is extremely brutal. Let me tell you something, you know what, let me stop because when you think it's peace and safety, it's sudden destruction. Sickness is a bitch for some parents but I know how sickness come about; thus try to live your life good and clean because there are evil forces out there.

Never wait until your parents is dead to tell them you truly love them. They cannot hear you and it will be truly too late for you. You know your parent and or parents are good, cleave to their goodness. I know some of you can't afford to take your parents out, but hug them and tell them you truly love them. Never deny your parent or parents the pleasure of them hearing you say these precious and good words. *I TRULY LOVE YOU AND THANK YOU FOR BEING MY PARENTS OR PARENT IF YOU ARE FROM A SINGLE PARENT HOUSEHOLD.*

I tell Lovey and my Mother they are my true and more than unconditional love of truth. They know this because I know they hear me; thus they are my sweet, sweet love. Trust me; I've given myself to them because all I can offer is the truth of me.

I know some of you are not touchy feely, but learn to hug your parents and or parent and spend time with them. It matters not if it's doing goofy and fun things. Never wait until it's too late. My mom and I did things together and I miss those things. I try doing things with my children, but since sickness has entered my life; we don't do as much, but I make sure I tell them have a good day when I can. I do tell them I love them lots but not often enough from my point of view.

I cherish Lovey and my Mother and you see this above with my dedication of Sweet Sweet Love by Christopher Martin. I wanted to change this song because many of you are saying he's talking about sexual relation with someone. For me I truly do not look at that. For many of you; sexual gratification is it and this song spells sexual gratification, but for me it's so much more. Making love is truly not about sexual relations from a spiritual standpoint. True love is truth and whichever way you look at it, giving Lovey and or your true loved ones your truth is sweet. It's sweet sweet love. For me connecting with Lovey and my mother this way is joy because I can dance with them my way. Giving them my truth and sharing my truth is my passion; truth, thus my sweet sweet love. When you find truth and truth love you don't want to let it go. You want to protect it each and every day. You cherish it and do all you can to keep this truth and truth love with you and within you.

True love has nothing to do with your pocket book; your financial gain or wealth; it has to do with truth, the preservation of honest and true life.

True love is going the distance despite the obstacles that come your way. You work on each obstacle together and you do overcome them. You cannot give up on truth despite your fears and tears come on now.

True love is holding hands and continually feeling the affection of the person you are with. That pure and raw energy the both of you emit for each other is beauty.

That energy maintains and sustains you. Lovey has been trying to show you this, but from a human standpoint we cannot comprehend or gravitate to this truth and it is so sad; truly sad.

True love is true guidance in a good and true way.

True love builds positively because neither one of you are trying to outdo each other. Yes tongue and teeth will meet. You will do things to get him or her jealous just to feel him or her beneath or atop of you and this is fine.

Trust me pissing him or her off at times can be a joy for the makeup, but never take someone else in the picture and or your relationship.

Yes it's hard for many. Some of you men feel that you must have dis oman and datday oman down the lane and they must produce a seed for you and this is truly wrong. No man can give his or her time to all his children equally if they have children for more than one woman or man. ***SOME CHILDREN ARE NEGLECTED; THUS YOU ARE A NEGLECTFUL FATHER.*** And don't go there and say, your wife is going to have to raise another woman's child. This is wrong. ***You were the infidel and she should not have to be punished for your willful sin and sins.***

Promiscuity is adultery and it is punishable by death.
And having children while married to another man or woman is wrong; a sin.

You committed adultery thus producing an adulterous and or sinful child. That child do not belong to Lovey, that child belong to death.

Please do not beat yourself up over this because there is forgiveness for adultery. Many of us do not know what constitutes adultery and no one out there is telling the true truth about this. Pray and or talk to Lovey and ask him for forgiveness because you truly do not know what constitutes adultery. Be honest with him and never lie to him. The sin and sins of adultery do pass on to your children, thus the hardships many of them face in their day to day lives.

Well my baby is well taken care of because my man is rich; you are gloating and harping on; saying.

Well koodles for you but your child is no exception to the rule. There is a global meltdown that is coming and many rich people including companies will lose it all.

The earth can no longer maintain and sustain the global elite (wicked) of this world. Thus the collapse of man and all that man created to rob and cheat each other must collapse; fall. When this happens many are going to die. And it matters not if it's death by starvation, poor drinking water, suicide, murder. Many are going to die.

I've told you in another book, the menu at some restaurants is going to read, now serving humans.

Cannibalism is going to become the norm; the true reality of man; humans.

Thus when you are married and in a relationship with your wife or husband and you knowingly have an affair you take on the sin and sins of him and her. So if he or she had one billion sin and you had one sin; you've added that billion sin of him and her to your slate. So if you were given a saving grace for that one sin you no longer have a saving grace because you added more sins to your record. And don't go there saying it's not fair. You sinned thus it is fair. You knowingly did something wrong thus you are faulted for your wrong.

Lovey doesn't give up on us; we are the ones to give up on him.

We are the ones to accept false deities over him.

We are the ones to listen to wicked and evil people and disgrace him.

We are the ones to think death is good when we know death cannot give life, death and only take life.

We are the ones to abandon truth for lies and when the lies do not work out, we are left holding the bag and running back to Lovey.

We are the ones to ignore all the warning signs without knowing them; the truth.

We are the ones to say Lovey would kill his own child to protect the wicked and evil.

*We are the ones to give away our lives and expect Lovey to rescue us in the end. Something Lovey cannot do because of **WILL; YOUR GOOD AND TRUE INCLUDING EVIL WILL.***

Lovey did not take your right from you; you gave it to someone that was not deserving of it.

Like I said, adultery is forgiven if you do not know the full truth. Some people know the truth but yet plunge head first into the sin. For this, there is no forgiveness for because your sin was willful.

Our life did not have to be so hard but because we wanted what the next man has, we elect to choose the folly ground and lose it all in the end.

What belongs to Mr. Jones or Mr. Wright belongs to them and you can't want it. You did not work hard to get your own so now that Mr. Jones and Mr. Wright has theirs why do you want it?

Did you work for it?

No. So why want theirs and not yours?

As for me, I will not fight anyone for their choice of death; religion or politics. As long as you do not come to my door selling me your shit and shitty gods I am fine. Your god is not mine so do not sell me yours. I am not selling you mine nor would I sell you my god because my god; truth cannot be bought or sold. And don't you dare think it with these books. Say it and let me bleeping school you rude and proper.

What's yours is truly yours and what Lovey has and have given me is truly mine. So stay the hell out of my way with your fraud and fraudulent gods.

When I am in need I do not see them nor do I want and need to see them. My way and life; good and true life and way is fine. And it is with this good and true life that I intend to live with when my spirit sheds the flesh; if my spirit sheds the flesh.

You cannot say you love God and believe in lies when it comes to him.

You cannot say you are a preacher and teacher but yet do the opposite of what you are to do. People trust you with all and you're the ones sending humanity to hell why?

Do you know the chaos that is going to be rained down on earth shortly?

Billions are going to lose their life because of you and your lies. Now tell me, was this called for knowing that you too are going to die?

All that the devil gave to you, you are going to lose it because evil keep the life of no one. Evil kill your life all around.

No human being is evil loyal to. Not even the people who are loyal to evil. EVIL IS ONLY LOYAL TO DEATH AND DEATH ONLY NOT HUMANS. EVIL IS SIN THUS THE EVIL AND EVILS AND OR SIN AND SINS THAT WE DO HAND US OVER TO DEATH TO DIE.

To the clergy and politicians of the world; globe, why deceive like this if you knew you could not handle the work you took up?

Do not pick up something you cannot handle. When you do, you are condemning self come on now.

Be true to you and the people you teach and preach to.

Truth cannot lie and we all know this. Yes there is a burden we all have to face, but that burden gets better over time come on now. As we grow life do get better for some.

No it doesn't and speak for yourself you are saying. Life does get better come on now.

I am in debt so shut the bleep up you are saying and yelling.

We are all in debt. As I am writing this book I am in debt. We all need help yes, but some of us are living above our means.

Some of us like to spend and not think of tomorrow.

Some of us cannot save because of the relationship and or relationships we are in.

Some of us are single parents and what you get cannot stretch. There are no baby daddies to say here I need help, help me. And if there are baby daddies around they truly don't help, so all the burden is on you. I know because I am there. I do for me and my children. Thus I truly love my brothers for the help they give me sometimes. My sister bless her as well because I do ask her for help when I am truly in need. But my brothers, I truly hope Lovey bless and keep them because they are my bright and morning star on certain days. I have to lift my hand on high for them. Yes my sister too but my brothers. Wow.

Oh Lord truly bless my brothers with every good blessing you can bestow upon them. They are my need and want here on earth; you and my mother too Lovey, but on this day my brothers and sister also. Trust me people my heart of goodness and truth go out to my two brothers on my mother's side. Lovey, in all you do, please prepare a good and true place with you for them as you've done my Mother. In all you do for me truly remember them and never let their light with you go dim. Lighten their load; burdens and save them for me. I truly love them unconditionally thus my life would not be the same without them. Bestow your blessing on my sister and never forget her but my brothers I will never forget because they are there for me unconditionally. Fam and people do not get me wrong; I truly love my sister, but my brothers hold a special place in my heart and this will never ever change.

Let me tell you something people, when you have good family members bestow blessings of truth on them. They are your hope and light as well. Never forget goodness and kindness.

Goodness is my sweet sweet love and all the good I do is my true love and love making. I will never get old when it comes to true giving if that makes any sense to you.

Wow. Thus I cling to Lovey and my Mother. I have to because at the end of the day, they are truly there for me. Hey they cannot give me financially, but they are there to protect me and I truly love that.

So in all I do, I have to save Lovey and my Mother; thus I tell you, don't come around me giving me your stinking god and gods including idols. I do not want nor do I need them. I am loyal and true to Lovey. I will not leave him for you and if yu come roune mi with di try my god bullshit, truss mi; di bawling wey mi du fi yu, hell cry because my tears with flood there with sulphuric acid if I can help it. Truss mi; Lovey betta get vex to di point where you are condemned right away for your bullshit when it comes to me and him. I do not joke when it comes to Lovey and me, so truly know what you are doing with me and Him Lovey including my Mother.

I truly don't play people. No, not my Lovey to Yass. Fimi Lovey. Yu waane tek mi from im? Wow because you truly do not know my hell that is outlined for you when you try this bullshit. And no matter how I tell him I am leaving him and divorcing him, he will not let me leave.

Thus I cannot comprehend nor can I over stand why some of these clergy people would do some of the things they do. ***If you are representing God, should you not represent him Lovey true?***

Should you not be true to him?

If Lovey is saving you, why are you doing wrong when it comes to him?

Why are you lying to humanity about him?

Why deceive?

Now tell me, what wrong did Lovey do to you for you to go against him like this? What wrong did life; Lovey do to you for you to go against life, Lovey like this?

Now let me ask you this. IF LOVEY IS YOUR ONE AND ONLY GOD; YOUR TRUE ONE AND ONLY, WHY ARE YOU CHEATING ON HIM?

You claim that Gad a Gad; soh why cheat on him with other gods?

Are you not telling God that you are nasty and you have no good and true will for him?

You claim to be clean, but you are dirty. You do dirty things then say God is going to forgive you. But how can God forgive willful sins; dirt?

How can God forgive you for spreading lies and hate against him?

How can God forgive you for taking his people away from him?

How can God forgive you and you've destroyed him, his people and this earth; all, including his character?

So now tell me, where is your foundation and framework with Lovey; God?

Where is your home and future with him?

Where is the home and future of your people and or congregation with him?

Tell me, where is it? Have you not condemned your congregation to hell including the family and or children of your congregation?

You ministered and fabricate stories for your own personal gain by telling lies on God, the God you say ordained you. How could you do this?

What lies did God; Lovey tell on you for you to tell lies on him so?

In all you've done, you've dirtied the content and character of Lovey and none of you are remorseful. Some of you go so far as...wow. You know what; let me stop here because your judgment I truly do not want to know or see, but I know it and see it.

Michelle

The spirit is down but my hope is strong. I have to be strong and continue to be strong. Can't let my problems get me down. There is only so much I can do and when the doing is done then all comes to an end. You count your loss and tomorrow you regroup again; go again until you can't go anymore.

Am I winning the battle?

No, but I cannot give up today. I do what I can until I cannot do anymore and tomorrow I go again.

Yes sometimes I wish I had an unlimited bank account but this is wishful thinking because I know my drought.

I don't even want to ask Lovey why because my head is on another level this morning. Damn I am so broke that I can't go to my appointment. Have bus fare to go but no bus fare to come back home. Can't even send my son to school because I have no money to buy tickets for him nor do I have money for him to buy lunch. Yes the school was helping me with bus tickets but with his poor attendance record and lateness I can't get help anymore. I've asked him to just go to school on time but with everything else, my words go through one ear and out the other. Little things that can help me, they truly don't do; thus I've said to myself, if I was to make it with these books, I would not let them inherit my fortune or Lovey's fortune. ***Well they cannot inherit Lovey's fortune because Lovey's fortune is for his good and true people and the land and lands they live in.*** Yes I know my children and their faults and they know mine. As parents, we kill ourselves for our children by working so hard for them, but when it comes to you and building you, many cannot do that.

For me I don't want big things from my children, it's the little things that can help me that matters. These things are what's important to me. The little things help me but they cannot see that thus I have some and or one that is bleeping miserly.

I cannot stand miserly people; I loathe and truly hate them; these type of people and I truly do not want to be around any. If you as a child see your parent struggling and you can help them truly help your parent if that parent was good to you.

I am not one to endorse bad parents; parents that exited out of your life and when they are old dem a look fi yu fi support dem. Dem neva gi yu nothing inna life, not even a pencil fi gaah school, but yet now that you've made it dem want sinting from yu. Kaka cauna to yass. How does that work?

You haven't done anything for me all my life and now that you are old and needy; you are looking to me for help?

No, I help the mother and granny that struggled to raise me. I help the aunt and uncle that batta batta fi raise me. You did not know me when I was growing up so truly don't know me when I am older because *I KNOW YOU NOT.*

So children if you are working and you see that your home need a bag or carton or jug of milk and you can afford to buy it, buy it. Don't let your parents have to ask you for help. Know what is needed in your household and buy it if you are working and can afford to. If you are not working and the laundry is piling up, do the laundry for your parents or parent. Help clean the house and take some of the burden and burdens off your parents or parent. If you have a car, pick up your siblings from day care and go grocery shopping for your parents or parent. Come on now. Parents and or your parent can't bare the burden and burdens of life alone.

If you can afford to put $10.00 in your mother's pocket each pay cheque, put it in her pocket. Tell her buy a coffee or tea with it.

If you can help to pay a bill for her if she's not charging you rent, pay that bill each month for her because at the end of the day you are taking some of the stress off her.

If you pay rent, say $200.00 per month and you can afford to buy groceries occasionally; buy her groceries like milk or toilet paper and tooth paste. $20.00 of necessary groceries is a great help trust me on this.

If you can't buy groceries then put a $10.00 or $20.00 in her pocket. She is there for you in all the good that you do, so truly be there for her too. ___I know some of you can't afford to do this, but a hug occasionally and telling her you appreciate and truly love her does not hurt.___

___Trust me some of us parents yearn this and crave this because good and true words do make our lives easier; worth living.___ As parents good words lift us up and make us proud. So not all is financial. So no, I will not ask Lovey why because just as how I am broke he is broke also. We are broke together and yes I have some wonderful music to lift up my spirit. I truly don't want to play them because I am too lazy.

It's a beautiful day and I am going to clean the kaka off my balcony because the water is gone again until 12 noon but we will see.

Hopefully I can wash about five pieces of clothes to hang them outside for the water to drip out of them when the water comes back. Yes I am real country people hence the hand washing is still in me. Family, my true family, you have to truly love life and bare on. *(And no I did not spell bare wrong. Bear is an animal in my book. And bare is my strength and perseverance; good will; good will to carry on.)*

It's harder than hell but I can't get upset today. It's not worth it and I am so not going to let my hardships get to me. I have to regroup and come again and no I refuse to bug my family. I have to face my hardships alone, hence I have these books for you to see that problems do come and they do go. In life do what you can but don't do what you cannot. I am a single parent and every single parent know it's not easy raising children by yourself. At times you are not financially able or capable. As for me I refuse to tun trouble to anyone, so I bare my burdens with Lovey because we are in the same boat together. If I am sinking Lovey is sinking with me.

If I am up, Lovey is up with me. Do I wish he can help us both out of this sinking ship or boat?

You bet your last dollar I do.

Do I feel like a failure at times?

Yes. More often than I want to. Failure do make you stronger but yet, failure weakens you over time. So yes failure is strength, but it is also weakness.

It's Monday November 16, 2015 and I am so needing this year to be over. So not looking forward to my birthday next month on this day. I don't know if it's because I was watching gang documentaries on the internet but my spirit is truly not right. My mind is so out of it today that I truly cannot think properly. Fam, my true family wow.

Wow; the coldness and heartlessness of some in society. How can another human being just live to kill?

No, because I truly do not comprehend why we as human beings need to find a place to belong.

WHAT PURPOSE DOES BELONGING SERVE?

NO, TRULY TELL ME, WHAT PURPOSE DOES BELONGING SERVE?

TRULY TELL ME, WHY DO WE HAVE TO LOOK FOR A PLACE TO BELONG?

Do we not belong to life and death already? So why want to belong someplace else?

I truly don't know because I truly cannot and will never comprehend why people belong in gangs; death.

I cannot comprehend what would make you hate yourself and another human being so; that you would be filled with so much hate and rage that you have to go out there and kill; create conflict and or harm in another human beings life?

Maybe it's me that cannot see the hate and rage in me. Like I said; I hate and loathe miserly people, thus if I make it I will not let my children inherit my fortune given the way they are now. But is that truly hate and loathsome? I need my children to freely give with a good heart. Not all my children are miserly with money and food and when I see positive changes in them, they will inherit my fortune ***but not Lovey's fortune.***

The ones that are miserly, I truly cannot live around and or with them. Therefore they are the ones that are left out and this is what I should have said above.

Fam, my truth is truly giving with a good and true heart; pure and clean heart, but it's not everyone that I truly want to give to; nor is it everyone that I am going to give to. My people and family which is Lovey's true people and family that is good and true I have to give to and try to save. I have to because Lovey is my true and unconditional love. He cannot bless me and I not share with his good and true people; Him. True love share without being greedy and miserly. Yes you can be greedy for Lovey, but you cannot be miserly. Hey when you love true you are greedy for the person that you truly love. You do all to protect each other and let each other rise. Hurt is not in the picture because you do not do anything to hurt your true love under any circumstance (s).

True love more than indefinitely does not want or need a controlled society. I certainly don't.

So no, I cannot comprehend gangs and the violence and death that is associated with them.

No Fam, how can someone grow so cold and heartless that they would murder another human being without remorse or regret?

Are the demons of hell this cold upon earth?

Do these people think of their soul and or spirit?

Do they even think of hell?

I don't know because I have to ask, ***what is life to some of you?***

IF YOU DO NOT VALUE LIFE, HOW CAN YOU VALUE SELF?

Yes I know many of you grew up in broken homes and in abusive homes. But at what point in life do you say fuck it, I don't care anymore and I am going to join a gang and become heartless like the bitch and bitches that abused me?

I know abuse, seen it and lived it, ***BUT I REFUSE TO LET ABUSE TIE ME DOWN.***

I REFUSE TO GIVE ABUSE THE VICTORY OVER ME.

ABUSE DEFINITELY DO NOT SHAPE ME OR MY LIFE; SO WHY WOULD I WANT TO GIVE INTO IT.

I REFUSE TO LET ABUSE STOP ME IN LIFE.
REFUSE TO BE DEFINED BY ABUSE.

REFUSE TO BUY INTO THE ABUSIVE STEREOTYPES.

I am my own woman and abuse isn't going to tell me how to raise my children or how to live. I have to rise above the ills and pain I faced; thus abuse isn't going to control me or my thoughts. I am more than better than that, thus I am living and doing all that is good and true for me and my children; family, come on now.

Abuse isn't going to alienate them (my children) or take them (my children) from me. Yes my children has and have seen abuse and experience abuse, but none has made abuse define them or stop them from achieving something in life.

Bad choices they've made friendship and relationship wise just like me, but abuse does not define them or shape their lives and it should not shape yours.

I will not buy into what society say is the norm because I AM TRULY NOT LOOKING FOR A PLACE OR HOME TO BELONG. I BELONG ALREADY, SO WHY SHOULD I BELONG SOMEPLACE ELSE?

Do you get what I mean?

I am right for me. I may not be right for you, but I am truly right for me and despite my hardships and pain; I truly love and respect me. I have my set and or values that I live by already, so why should I let you change me to please you? ___SO I WILL NOT BUY INTO THE I AM A PRODUCT OF ABUSE THEREFORE I AM THE WAY I AM.___

No, I refuse to buy into this because after the pain and hurt is gone; over, you are free.

We are angry and anger do turn into hate but what we as people forget is that; ___YOU HAVE THE FATE OF YOUR ABUSER IN YOUR HAND. YOU HOLD HIM OR HER LOCKED IN HELL AND YOU CAN KEEP THAT PERSON IN HELL FOREVER EVER WITHOUT END. THUS I TELL YOU I WORRY NOT ABOUT MY ENEMIES BECAUSE THERE IS AN APP FOR THEM AND THAT APP IS HELL.___

For some of you this is so what; I want justice, but I tell you; the hell they face, they will be burning like a bitch crying out to you for forgiveness and none is given. So no, I do not govern my life by my struggles. These struggles are lessons we can all learn from including our children.

Why should I do all that is evil with you just to belong to your elite group of Satanists; evil and wicked demons of people; hell? You concern me not because I know your hell and death. You've forgotten this but I've not forgotten it. So truly do you and leave me out of your crap and bullshit.

Why should I have to accept your false and stinking cesspools of gods and goddesses just to eat and or belong in your group?

I AM ME, SO WHY ARE YOU CHANGING ME TO PLEASE YOU?

I don't know you or your god, so don't come into my world and take and or steal my truth from me.

Your loathsome creep of gods and goddesses did not create this earth and universe, but yet I am to give up my life for them and they are bleeping dead and gone and can't do a damned thing here on this earth?

They are dead; earth is dying, but yet they cannot save earth from you and your lies; their lies.

Say it so I can blast you. I know life, thus humans are slated to die globally before 2032. Death cannot give life, thus death is slated to die. Even you know this but yet you put death over life and say one man is going to come and save you.

No man can save you from your sins if they are not ordained to by Lovey.

So truly good luck to billions of you because I know the truth and true love of Lovey when it comes to his beloved and true people. Lovey would never sacrifice or kill his children for death. Yes death is a god, thus death kills; sacrifice his people unto to him literally.

It's been a long day and I've been up and down on the board on the internet. Thus I have to ask, what are some of the uber rich going to do when the economies of the globe collapse?

What are their children going to do?

Oh well this is me when I am confused and my head begins to hurt from over thinking. Yes I do over think because my brain is on a different level at times.

Now I am going to ask you this, WHAT IS SO BAD ABOUT THE SWASTIKA? Isn't the swastika the number 55 encrypted; your east, west, north and south; more specifically your North and South Pole?

One can say 45, but if you look carefully it's fifty five. But either way both numbers represent death and are the numbers of death not life and goodness.

Whereas nine represent divinity; meaning there is no number greater than nine. No, not 13 but nine.

Nine is the final number in life thus you are told cats have nine lives. So no, one cannot live beyond nine cycles of life here on earth with each cycle being 100 years. And truly don't come to me with Adam lived over 900 years because no man can or could live beyond 900 years; nine cycles.

Impossible, thus know the truth come on now. **NO ONE THAT IS OF SIN AND OR COMMITTED SIN CAN PASS 9 CYCLES OF LIFE.** Thus 9 is the greatest number in the cycle of life; human life here on earth. *And yes, I now know why Africa cannot let go of her European own due to poles.*

Michelle

It's November 17th and the dreams kept coming this morning. Last night and this morning I was I talking to Lovey about the number 9. Wow because I so did not get a complete 8 hours of sleep. My head hurt, not with confusion, but with lack of comprehension. Somehow I think I am wrong when I said life cycles come in increments of 100. I truly don't know why I feel 10 is the appropriate increments. Thus 9 is the highest form and or level of life and no number is greater than nine.

I am not expecting you to comprehend this because numerology is simple but confusing to some.

In numerology the highest and or greatest number you can get is 9 and the process repeats itself again. So nine is the only true finite number out there. Some may say infinite but 9 is not continuous. When you get to the ninth level, the process repeats again. For example 999 is 9+9+9 =27 now add 2+7 and you get nine.

Well what about 1000?

1000 equals one. 1+0+0+0 = 1

So there are no levels beyond nine and can never be because after nine, the process of life starts again. Thus no one can live beyond and or past nine cycles. No, it does not mean you stop living, it just means the cycle of life starts at one again. Yes this is hard for me to explain because I am just figuring it out. It is complicated but yet simple. And yes some people will dispute this.

So please do not frustrate your brain trying to figure this out or you will go mad; insane.

Nine degrees and or the ninth cycle of life has to do with cleanliness of thought and self.

When you've reached the ninth degree of life and you are a female your thoughts are pure and void of sin.

WHEN YOU ARE AT THIS STAGE OF LIFE, MEN ARE NOT INVOLVED AND THE THOUGHT OF BEING WITH A MALE BECOMES UNCLEAN; MAKE YOU UNCLEAN.

If you think of a man at this level; level nine, you become dirty; unclean and you have to go back to level one. At this stage you have to become clean again and the process is truly not easy. This I found out last night and or this morning. And in truth I don't know if I've explained this level right but this explanation is the best I can do. Here your life is devoted to cleanliness and truth and this is why you see monks and nuns living alone and void of seminal exchange with males and females. *And yes I am truly sorry Lovey to bring these people; monks and nuns into this because this is not a religious thing, but I had to for example purpose only.*

These people truly have nothing to do with you due to beliefs; religion. The 9th level of life is pure but our thoughts of unification with the opposite sex defile and or contaminate us. So no human can live beyond nine cycles which is 900 years. This has to do with flesh and cleanliness and not so much the spirit. Yes the spirit is both energy and flesh and the spirit must accommodate both, but once you move into the spiritual realm this cycle change. So nine is limited in every which way. Thus our life is limited here on earth.

This changes when you get to the spiritual realm. And this depend on the life you lived in the living. If your life is evil and or you lived a unclean and wicked life here on earth, **_you cannot move on to greater life._** *You must go down to see DEATH AND THE DEMONS OF HELL. THEREFORE, YOUR TRIANGLE IS VERY IMPORTANT IN THE PHYSICAL WORLD.* Many of you can change your downward triangle to the upright triangle if you know your sins. Yes some sins cannot be forgiven and they are automatic death here on earth, but truly do not give up. Strive for goodness. We all become dirty at some point in our lives. I'm back to level one in the cycle of life. I reached nine cycles but because I write intimate stories in the living in my head, I dirtied myself and had to go back to level one. Like I said, at this stage you cannot bring unification with someone into this process. There are no unification stage here because the ninth cycle is not governed by the flesh and or a combination of flesh and spirit. This level is governed by truth, the truth of life; pure cleanliness, your true you which is your good and true spirit. At this level, life begin a new and there are no limits to you if you are good and true. There are no limits to good and true; clean life on this level. I do not want to say this is the level of God because Lovey truly has no levels and true life is not governed by time.

Death is governed by time and it is us as humans that put time limits to everything.

And please don't ask me because no one can recycle their life. Meaning, you never live a life before this one no matter what people try to tell you.

Truly don't because you are sinning self and the people that say they've lived in a previous lifetime are blaspheming and sinning self.

No one die and come back as a animal or a plant or another human.

Don't because some of us can see hell and some of us do go into hell. We are observers only. We tell you what hell and the past look like. I've shown you and told you that we can dream in the past.

I've shown you if you are of truth and walking on the pathway of truth, you will be shown things like the creation of life and the first human being.

I've shown you how evil and or the evil dead can make you think they are alive. Thus some of you will think you've lived a past life when you have not.

No, I am not taking away from your experience, but I am clarifying you. Different people have different gifts but you have to be careful of your gift; thus strive and know truth. Not all in the spiritual realm are true and I've shown and told you this. Men are bitch niggas in the spiritual realm for me because they do lie and I've shown and told you this.

Yes I am off course and I am truly sorry.

So after discovering the truth about the number 9 I dreamt I was at a reunion. The venue was predominantly black but you had White and Chinese there. I was sitting at this table and I didn't know anyone there. They were going row by row for you to get up and get something to eat and speak, but my row didn't get up in time and the next row behind me quickly got up and went in line causing a jam up and or pile up of black people of my age.

I don't know what happened but I saw an old friend from high school Debbie Latham and Avalon Dixon come in and I went to say hi but Avalon gave me the cold shoulder. She frowned at me as if saying; I don't know you so do not approach me. Shi too good fi mi. Some a wi black people know how some a wi tan when wi get and or have status. The cold shoulder she gave me, I saw Debbie and I ran to hug her and we both cried. Debbie was dressed in blue and she was apologizing to me for something and I told her it was okay. We ended up at the top of the line where food was and for some strange reason there was this baby, beautiful baby there and I picked up the baby who is of light complexion.

I had her in my arms carrying her. You could also see the snacks that you could take for yourself. Oh, I forgot; at the entrance there was this elder Chinese lady and she said, everyone forgot about her and I said no we didn't and she got so excited and smiled.

I think this is a dream in a dream and maybe I am going to have a new beginning soon. I will not try to figure out this dream, so I am so going to leave it alone.

Dreamt I was in a argument. I was in this place with all young white males and females. I would say late teens to very early twenties. Some of the teens were Goth because they had piercings and some had jet black hair. They were converting to Islam and the varieties of Islam. Some were Christian Muslims, Muslims and what have you.

They were so pissed off at me because of my views on God; Lovey I believe. To them I guess God and or Lovey is a religion and I had no talk when it came to God and or Lovey. I was changing their views I guess. But with all that being said, none of them knew God and or Lovey so I asked, ***"IF GOD WAS A RELIGION, WHAT RELIGION IS HE,"*** and no one could answer me. Not one could tell me what religion Lovey is. So if you truly don't know, why are you walking in the way of the wicked? Should you not walk away from the wicked and live by your truth as given by Lovey himself?

SHOULDN'T PSALMS ONE BE YOUR KEEP AND STRIVE IN THE PHYSICAL AND SPIRITUAL WORLD?

Dreamt I was somewhere in the United States and George Bush the son was running for office again. He was campaigning with his Vice President. I am thinking Ross Perot but it isn't him from his Google picture.

This Vice President had straight nose. None of the Vice Presidents match the picture I am looking for. And I cannot go through the list of actors out there. Don't have to. The original teacher Mr. Feeny is what this man looked like. He did not want to become Vice President but he was running anyway. I guess he wanted to get votes and then at the right time quit and give his votes to George Bush (the son). But what I found odd in the dream was there were two jugs and they were both identical in colour and size. I don't know if this is a colour but the colour was a fiery orange red. The jugs were red and I don't think anyone could see these jugs a part from me. There was a lot of people that was with George Bush on his campaign because a lot of people came out to see what he had to say. And yes the Mr. Feeny's lookalike told me he did not want to run for Vice President. In the dreams there were issues they

America did not seem to have answers for, like immigration and some other issues that plagued them like terrorism. I don't know what I said, but I know I was not liked and this one White Lady in a green top said something to me. I know the question was what would you do? Meaning what I would do if I was the president of the United States.

I told her I would limit immigration to certain countries and walked away from her.

Also dreamt Russia in yellow. It's as if ALL OF EUROPE WAS RUSSIA.

There were no Spain, no France, no Portugal and no other European lands apart from Mongolia and China.

All other lands were not there. I cannot tell you if Japan and North and South Korea were there, **_but I know Africa was there. So it was Africa, Russia, Mongolia and China._** *I could not see more because my bladder acted up and I had to get up and go to the washroom. So I truly do not know what is going to happen in Russia but the land mass of Russia was massive; more massive than it is now and in yellow.* **_And no there was no Tajikistan, Azerbaijan, Turkmenistan, Ukraine, Georgia just one massive land space that was Russia._**

There are more dreams but somehow I cannot remember them right now. If I do I will include them in this book or another book. So if you can make sense out of any of these dreams, please by all means go ahead.

Those red jugs, drinking jugs or pitcher wow. I am so staying out of the politics of the United States people because something is truly not right in the political arena there and I am so staying out of their political struggles and troubles.

They need to fix their own problem and problems. And like I said in another book,

YOU CANNOT MAKE FRIENDS WITH YOUR ENEMY; NO ONE CAN.

SO I TRULY DON'T KNOW WHY NATIONS ARE MAKING NICE WITH THEM. YOUR ENEMY IS YOUR ENEMY AND YOU'RE ENEMIES FOR MORE THAN LIFE COME ON NOW.

Your enemy is your enemy and all too often countries side with the enemy only to lose it all in the end. And no I am not dropping words. IF YOU HAVE NO GOOD WILL WHEN IT COMES TO ME, WHY THE HELL WOULD I WANT OR NEED TO BEFRIEND YOU? You've caused my people and country severe pain; stay the hell away from me because I am truly not going to make nice with you when all comes crashing down on you. I am going to remember the pain and suffering you caused my land and people, so stay in your damned hell; condemned land. My responsibility now is to ensure my people are safe and well fed; secure in all that is going to come. WW3 is inevitable, so do you and I will continue to do for me and my people including land.

I don't need your sympathy, nor do I need your resources. You've put sanctions on me and at the final hour when your economy is going to collapse you want to trade with me; make nice with me and lift your embargo. Embargo you put on my country to let my people go hungry so that we would come your way.

**Well no, bleep you.** The road is rough but trust me it does get better over the long haul. All that you do to eliminate me and get lands to side against me by joining you will come back to haunt you and them because with death, its death for death and you did do me wrong.

THUS NO LAND ON THE FACE OF THIS EARTH IS DEMOCRATIC; ABSOLUTELY NONE.

Well I live in a democratic land.

No you do not because you are truly not free and your land wage war; strife with other lands. So your land is truly not democratic. Your land is a bully that seeks to dominate, control, enslave and influence freedom and free speech in another land. They have you the citizen controlled and brainwashed thus your land is truly not liked by anyone. *__There is no true freedom of speech because if you speak out and speak the truth you are set up and killed.__* Thus there is no such thing as free speech and freedom in so called democratic lands.

__To the politicians of the world, who the fuck are any of you to tell me what I can and cannot do in my land?__

Bleep you. Your people are not my people, so truly do not tell me how to govern my people. Your people have no say; so why the fuck do you think you can come into my land and tell me what to do? Govern your damned land and pay down your bleeping national debt so death can take your land and people off his and her status of doom record; death record. You're all death's pawn so pawn this (the middle finger) and learn.

As long as I am providing for my people and ensuring their needs are met and provided for in a good way, don't interfere. Your land is broke and corrupt; hell bound, so truly stay out of my affairs because you are not needed and I will not listen to you. However, I will learn and teach my people not to become like any of you. I will teach them not to side with death because when you do, your economy collapse and death will walk in the most violent of ways upon land; our land. Death will take at will and we see this globally today.

So truly look at the debt load of your country, the death toll of your people; citizens globally and tell me if your people can pay back this sinful debt. ***You owe debt more than me, so who are you the broke ass and asses of the world to talk, dictate to me.***

I make peace, I do not strive to kill or steal; make war so bleep off and stay in your own dead and debt filled continent; land. Death owns you not me so bleep off and breeze off.

Why should anyone listen to you when TRUE PEACE IN TRULY NOT IN YOU. You're all the bleeping puppets of Babylon thus they breed in your land and lands then turn around and exterminate the lots of you like cockroaches.

So now Lovey, Why?

Why subject us including you my beloved to the evils and wickedness of man; humanity?

This dream I forgot. Dreamt about Will I Am of the Black Eyed Peas. This dream is weird because I truly cannot understand it. He had two girls; both black. One dark and the other not so dark but not too brown. The dark skinned or black one was sheer sex; she gave him the pleasure he needed. The not so dark one was his main squeeze I guess. So he had these two girls on the go and neither one knew about each other. I can't fully remember what happened but he hid the dark one under this black chair that was like a car seat. The not so dark one was coming and he did not want to get caught. But before that happened we were in this car and I took a seat in the back. The seat was black and he was driving me somewhere. I believe I did not want to go with him but he said what he had to do won't take long. So we went to this building. He had something like a parachute jet pack of yellow and he used it to get to the top floor of the building where this female was, but the jet pack did not go up. He tried again and failed. In the dream it seemed like he had to do something for this female and the relationship was not sexual. His sexual conquest had to do with the two black females. It was after doing his jet pack stunt that the two black females came into play. And that was all my dreams for this morning.

Michelle

My God My God why have you forsaken me?

Allelujah, have mercy because Bob (Bob Marley) was right when it said, "THERE AIN'T NO USE, NO ONE CAN STOP THEM NOW," in his song Real Situation.

Dear God; Lovey why forsake me and humanity like this? This man was warning us and he told us it doesn't make any sense for us to try.

The devil won Lovey.

The devil won and I am on the verge of tears to what I just saw. It's 3:32 am November 18, 2015 and I am writing because I can't go back to sleep. I don't know if I was in hell Lovey but I was underground somewhere walking with the current President of the United States Barak Obama. He said nothing to me and I said nothing to him. *In his face he had this red patch and or marking in his forehead with this light in the background. I don't think he knew that I saw the patch but as we walked on I saw the full marking in his forehead.*

The marking were 3 marks that resembled the markings on the Monster Energy Drink can but without the buffy part that resemble a 7 at the top. This was the mark in red with a light in Barak Obama's forehead. The markings are big and from my angle the marking covered a large portion of the right side of his forehead.

In the dream when I saw that, I had to get away from this man because I was not sure what he was capable of. Walking ahead and trying to escape I did not realize demons was in the place we were. I called out Allelujah and something round moved in the corner where it was perched and or sat. You see how gargoyles perch on a building, this is how this demon sat in the corner out of sight. I said Allelujah again and it rocked him. Allelujah was my protection but I had to keep saying Allelujah.

People wow because you see some of these depictions of creatures in movies and you truly have to wonder.

This thing was short and gross. His teeth were like the mask of Bane in Batman. Have mercy Lord, Allelujah.

Wow because the tears want to come again. Suffice it to say, I got out of the place I was at without injury; harm.

When I got through the door that was of a white creamy colour, the demon tried to get out but could not because the door closed back on him.

So now I can't go back to sleep because this dream scares me. I truly do not believe in the Anti Christ but with what I saw how can I not.

Was this hell I was in people, Fam?

Was this hell I was in with this man?

He had no smile on his face; he was just a man walking in his black clothing with the mark of death in his forehead. **_I see so many different things but to see this is truly beyond me._**

I figured out the Jesus thing but now seeing this I am scared shitless. I was truly not expecting this man; a Kenyan to sell out Kenya and the black race like this.

Now the other demon is set to visit Kenya.

So now Kenya is gone and the tears come because I had hope and good thought; Will of goodness for Kenya and the Kenyan people.

So now I have to ask you Lovey, did the government of Kenya sell land and people out?

Is this the final betrayal on black people's part; the black man?

Is this WHITE AND BLACK DEATH JOINING FORCES TO FURTHER DESTROY MAMA AFRICA?

Dear God Lovey have mercy because I feel it. I needed Kenya to stay pure and true to you. Yes I could be wrong; they are not going to side with the devil, but Lovey, **_WHAT BLACK LAND HAS AND HAVE TRULY KEPT YOU?_**

Fam and people, Kenya is that old and I've told you, the spear in the Kenyan Flag is what kills Death; White Death in the spiritual realm. So to have Black and White Death visit this land truly do not sit well in my stomach.

Wow because I am grieving Lovey because humanity is screwed literally now. Absolutely nothing can stop the devil here on earth not even you.

We lost Lovey because my life is truly not my own. This man was ordained to take the seat of the United States Lovey and he turned against truth; humanity like this?

He was to save America not kill it.

How could he hand America over to death on a silver platter like this?

Lovey I cannot correlate this dream to the red pitchers because I truly don't want to. Thus I ask you WHY Lovey?

Why did we as humans fail self including you?

I am weak and scared for my life and the life of my family now. Hope is gone and the tears come.

How can man; a man, any man hand over humanity to death on a silver platter like this?

How can we deceive ourselves into thinking that all is well?

But then Bob Marley told us, "when we think it's peace and safety its sudden destruction."

I truly did not see this coming Lovey and it hurts to know a Kenyan could do this. Mama Africa asked for prayer Lovey and I gave it to her. She's tired and I'm tired too, but to know a man; an African and or of African descent could deceive like this in the final hour hurts. It hurts man. I don't care if he's of mixed lineage because no one is seeing his mixed lineage. But why Lovey, why?

Why us the black race?

I know why Mama, Mother Africa let go of her North and South American own, but to have this final betrayal in the final hour hurts.

I am hurting to know that man have and has turned earth into a war zone of lies and deceit; sin. Lovey, it's gone on for too long. How do I save me, my family, the good seed and seeds you've given me?

How do I save you Lovey because I could not give you the home you needed? How do I reach out to you now?

I have no ark to give you to say, save my own; you. I too have failed and this hurts. *I CANNOT PRESERVE GOOD AND TRUE LIFE LOVEY BECAUSE THE DEVIL WON OVER MAN.*

THIS IS THE FINAL COUNTDOWN AND EVERY HUMAN BEING MUST NOW PAY WITH THEIR LIVES.

HELL IS NOW GOING TO BE UNLEASHED ON EARTH AND THERE IS ABSOLUTELY NOTHING ANYONE CAN DO ABOUT THIS.

I can't save the people of earth Allelujah because I can't even save me.

You know it's funny, you gave me the sword to kill Satan and a black man took it away. I know blood is not to be on my hands but did he truly kill Satan with it; the sword Lovey?

Did he Lovey?

Now tell me, what good am I in seeing all these things and can't save us, my family including brothers and sister, our good and true seed; you?

*I am scared Lovey thus I am coming to you with my fears. In all I've seen I've shown humanity; told them, **but to see this I cannot stomach.***

Anyone else but him, but it is him and no one else.

LIVES ARE GOING TO BE LOST LOVEY. OH MY GOD, MY GOD, WHY HAVE YOU FORSAKEN ME?

WHY HAVE YOU FORSAKEN ME LOVEY?

WHY HAVE YOU ABANDONED ME?

WHY LEAVE YOUR PEOPLE TO DIE?

You see me trying but have done nothing to help me save our people. Now I feel hopeless and condemned; lost for all eternity with what I saw with Barak. He was always the pawn Lovey we know this, but to see this. No, my stomach cannot take it. Thus no doors were open to me in the spiritual realm.

All doors were closed, thus *LIFE MEANS NOTHING ON EARTH. ABSOLUTELY NO LIFE MATTERS AND THIS DREAM PROVES IT. BLACK LIVES DON'T MATTER, WHITE LIVES DON'T MATTER AND CHINESE LIFE DON'T MATTER. THE ONLY THING OR LIFE THAT MATTERS IS BABYLONIAN LIFE; THE FEEDING OF DEATH WHEN IT COMES TO HUMANS; HUMANITY.*

We fed death, now death is truly going to take us on a massive scale literally and real soon.

This man is in hell Lovey and I was in his hell with him. Lovey is this his spiritual hell. Oh Allelujah have mercy on us all because hell has come to earth literally.

Why did you show me this Lovey?
Why did I have to see this?

Why him when he was ordained?

Allelujah, Allelujah, Allelujah have mercy because as humans we truly do not know what we have done.

It hurts Lovey, it hurts. Yes I am in tears because it hurts. Why us?

Why?

I know you are God Lovey but why?

Why did we have to fail you Lovey?

Now I ask you, why did you ask me to write you a book not once but twice?

WHY DID WE HAVE TO LISTEN TO THE LIES OF MEN?

NOW BILLIONS ARE GOING TO DIE.

Yes I want and need to see wicked and evil people gone from earth, but why him Lovey?

Now I ask you, is the book of man; their so called nasty book fulfilled?

Is it done now?

The show Lovey I have to cancel. I cannot do it. I am truly going to stay home because I have concerns and I am going to follow you. This is truly not the avenue for me and this is also what you are showing me. And the show was cancelled peopled. Courtney called me to cancel it. He was at a funeral.

With what I saw I have to talk to you about the safety of my family; brother. I cannot bare anymore burdens Lovey. I truly cannot and you know this.

Lovey I need you right now. I need you I need you I need you because I can't go on after this dream.

Yes I dreamt about me being in school, college, but to see this dream with him, I am scared because the Barak dream was a dream in a dream and I know this now as of November 20, 2015.

Lovey you know the evils of man and I refuse to die or be a sacrifice for anyone. You know the elimination that they do here on earth. Thus I worry not about them nor do I worry about the wicked and evil of society; humanity. Punishment comes and no one can blame the next land for slaughtering your ass. ***Your government gave death TOTAL JURISDICTION OVER YOU.***

SO NOW THAT YOU ARE PAYING THE PRICE YOU ARE CRYING BLOODY MURDER.

AS HUMANS, WE ALL KNOW THAT WHEN YOU INVITE THE DEVIL AND THEIR PEOPLE INTO OUR LAND AND LANDS; HOME, DESTRUCTION IS WHAT YOU GET. YOU ARE ELIMINATED BY ANY MEANS NECESSARY.

DEATH AND DESTRUCTION IS BY ANY MEANS NECESARRY AND THE ENEMY DID TELL YOU THIS. Malcolm X.

SO FROM THE DEVIL SET UP SHOP (Mosques, Temples, Shrines, Churches and what have you) IN YOUR LAND; HOME, YOU SHOULD HAVE KNOWN DEATH COMES.

TO THEM THE WICKED AND EVIL OF THIS WORLD, NO LIFE MATTERS AS LONG AS THE ONE HAS TOTAL DOMINATION AND CONTROL. Evil created global societies for themselves, but what wicked and evil people do not fully comprehend is that all they do for death, they too are going to die. Death is truly not loyal to any of them thus death take them as well.

AS FOR ME, I CANNOT LIVE IN A WORLD LIKE THIS WHERE I DO NOT HAVE A SAY; TRUE FREEDOM.

LOVEY, WE BOTH KNOW THAT THERE IS NO SUCH THING AS DEMOCRACY HERE ON EARTH BECAUSE ALL IS NOT TRULY PEACEFUL.

Human lives are not valued and this is truly a shame. Yes it would be nice if true peace can come for me and my children; family, you and my mother and the good and true seeds you have and as given me. Yes, let death and their children truly go because the time has truly come for death to go from us here on earth, in the universe and spiritual realm more than indefinitely and forever ever without end.

Democracy does not exist here on earth. We kill each other and muzzle people when they speak the truth. Some are killed. ***So tell me, what democratic society we live in if we live to kill and HUMAN LIFE VALUES NOTHING?***

I do not want to get caught up in the RAT RACE (Bob Marley) of it all. I chose life, good and true life for me, my family, children, you Lovey, my Mother and the good and true seeds you've given me including my great grandmother and grandmother.

Lovey, what do I truly do now because I truly do not know?

How do I move on from this dream?

Yes I am coming to you but the heart is heavy, truly heavy and my stomach is acting up with hunger pains.

Maybe I am not to think of this dream but let it be.

But with all this said Lovey, I have to come to you with all my concerns. I know you truly do not want me to walk this road and I have to adhere to you. I truly do love you and I do trust you Lovey, but doubt has set in again because of this dream.

I am truly sorry to doubt you because I was not expecting this given what I saw with Russia. So now Lovey, let me ask you this; is all of the North and South America going to sink; disappear and leave only Russia, Africa, Mongolia and China? Is North and South America going to be destroyed including the Caribbean?

No, not the Caribbean because you want your home in the Cayman Islands. So no, not all of the Caribbean will be destroyed.

Lovey, what do all of these dreams mean?

I cannot figure anything out on this day because I am confused. Oh Lovey, only you know and I am so going to leave all in your good and capable hands including my life, the life of my family and children including the life of the good and true seeds you've given me.

You are Allelujah and you know best.

Please continue to open my eyes to the full truth Lovey because I truly don't know what to think anymore.

Oh Lovey before I go; did the European nation give Jamaica 4.2 billion Euros to combat buggary?

If so Lovey, where did that 4.2 billion Euros go?

4.2 billion Euros could have paid off a portion of Jamaica's debt to the IMF come on now.

Now I ask you this, where did Andrew Holness get 250 million Jamaican to be building a Mega Mansion in Beverly Hills Jamaica?

I know it's not my concern Lovey but truly look into it. The people of Jamaica are suffering but yet he has this kind of money to spend on himself. So hoo much money im did a mek so as Prime Minister of Jamaica? People are dying and living in substandard housing, some can't afford medical care and food and im ha sumuch money fi a build a massive house suh? Buoy di people dem inna Jamaica fool fool to yass. Lovey what about the 18 babies that died in hospital care out there? Who's going to talk for them? Come on now.

Michelle

MY MUSICAL SELECTIONS:

DEXTA DAPS
SCARED TO LOVE

LADY RUDY
YOUR LOVE IS REAL

CHRISTOPHER MARTIN
NA NA NA
FIWI ISLAND
SWEET SWEET LOVE
UNDER THE INFLUENCE

KHAGO
BATTLEFIELD

BABY MARLEY

To me this CD is truly not for babies but for adults. Its calming and a nice house serenade but on what and or which day, I truly don't know.

Cloudy or rainy day, could be Sunday or your nightly lullaby. Yes this lullaby is experimental, missing what I truly don't know.

Can the melody take you away?

Yes, to a different world, but what world I truly don't know. So Baby Marley yes and no and quite unsure but yes anyway.

This CD is a challenge and I truly love challenges. So yes I am going to endorse. Buffalo Soldier mix can and will take you away if you just listen carefully.

JULIAN MARLEY
LEMME GO

BUGLE
MOVE DEM featuring Julian Marley

JO MERSA MARLEY ROCK AND SWING AND SKIP MARLEY CRY TO ME. These two young man to me are up and coming Marley's and I am looking to see how they do over time

VETERANS OF REGGAE AND DANCEHALL

Thus the sweet sounds of Reggae music more than need to come back. So I am going back to the past and endorse these veterans with the hopes that these now a days artists learn something from them and change the crap they are handing to people; society and calling it music. People don't need to listen to shit anymore, so if I can, I release society from the crap of shit you're all giving them and calling it music. Some a unnu caane DJ or sing. All some a unnu ha a gun an front. So now it's time to bury the lots of you because your music is a disease, infected with serious STD's. An di gun wey some a unnu poise up need to be buried with the lots of you. So let me take a page outta Ninga Book. No, I can't with the reverse the hearse. Im DJ it best.

GREGORY ISAACS
BANG BELLY

SUPER CAT
BOOPS
DEM DON'T WORRY WE featuring Heavy D

TIGER
NO WANGA GUT
This song is dedicated to some a unnu wanga gut gyal dem wey lay dung with this producer and that producer to get and maintain your career. Yes some a unnu man tu because batty nuh refuse nothing nowadays.

WHEN
BAM BAM
NO PUPPY LOVE

FRANKIE PAUL
SARAH

WORRIES IN THE DANCE
I KNOW THE SCORE
SLOW DOWN
STUCK ON YOU
CASANOVA
ALIESHA
SISTER NANCY
BAM BAM
ONE TWO

Special shout out to LADY ANN AND SISTER CHARMAINE. Man these ladies still have it. I have not included any songs for them because I'm trying to develop a episodic book that will include them, Lady Ann, Sister Charmaine, Frankie Paul and the songs of Gregory Isaacs.

Don't know how it will pan out. Started the book but I have to complete the Michelle Jean books before I can fully dedicate myself to this episodic book.

Michelle

OTHER BOOKS BY MICHELLE JEAN

Blackman Redemption – The Fall of Michelle Jean
Blackman Redemption – After the Fall Apology
Blackman Redemption – World Cry – Christine Lewis
Blackman Redemption
Blackman Redemption – The Rise and Fall of Jamaica
Blackman Redemption – The War of Israel
Blackman Redemption – The Way I Speak to God
Blackman Redemption – A Little Talk With Man
Blackman Redemption – The Den of Thieves
Blackman Redemption – The Death of Jamaica
Blackman Redemption – Happy Mother's Day
Blackman Redemption – The Death of Faith
Blackman Redemption – The War of Religion
Blackman Redemption – The Death of Russia
Blackman Redemption – The Truth
Blackman Redemption – Spiritual War
Blackman Redemption – The Youths
Blackman Redemption – Black Man Where Is Your God?

The New Book of Life
The New Book of Life – A Cry For The Children
The New Book of Life – Judgement
The New Book of Life – Love Bound
The New Book of Life – Me
The New Book of Life – Life

Just One of Those Days
Book Two – Just One of Those Days
Just One of Those Days – Book Three The Way I Feel
Just One of Those Days – Book Four

The Days I Am Weak
Crazy Thoughts – My Book of Sin
Broken
Ode to Mr. Dean Fraser

A Little Little Talk
A Little Little Talk – Book Two

Prayers
My Collective
A Little Talk/A Time For Fun and Play
Simple Poems
Behind The Scars
Songs of Praise And Love

Love Bound
Love Bound – Book Two

Dedication Unto My Kids
More Talk
Saving America From A Woman's Perspective
My Collective the Other Side of Me
My Collective the Dark Side of Me
A Blessed Day
Lose To Win
My Doubtful Days – Book One

My Little Talk With God
My Little Talk With God – Book Two

A Different Mood and World – Thinking

My Nagging Day

My Nagging Day – Book Two
Friday September 13, 2013
My True Love
It Would Be You
My Day

A Little Advice – Talk
1313, 2032, 2132 – The End of Man
Tata

MICHELLE'S BOOK BLOG – BOOKS 1 – 22

My Problem Day
A Better Way
Stay – Adultery and the Weight of Sin – Cleanliness
Message

Let's Talk
Lonely Days – Foundation
A Little Talk With Jamaica – As Long As I Live
Instructions For Death
My Lonely Thoughts
My Lonely Thoughts – Book Two
My Morning Talks – Prayers With God
What A Mess
My Little Book
A Little Word With You
My First Trip of 2015
Black Mother – Mama Africa
Islamic Thought
My California Trip January 2015
My True Devotion by Michelle – Michelle Jean
My Many Questions To God

My Talk
My Talk Book Two
My Talk Book Three – The Rise of Michelle Jean
My Talk Book Four
My Talk Book Five
My Talk Book Six
My Talk Book Seven
My Talk Book Eight – My Depression
My Talk Book Nine – Death
My Talk Book Ten – Wow
My Day – Book Two
My Talk Book Eleven – What About December?
Haven Hill
What About December – Book Two
My Talk Book Twelve – Summary and or Confusion
My Talk Book Thirteen
My Talk Book Fourteen – My Talk With God
My Talk Book Fifteen – My Talk
My Thoughts – Freedom
My Heart to Heart With Lovey – God

Letters to my song and words of praise and truth; My true and unconditional Love; Lovey, Good God and Allelujah

Caged